The Addict

a terrible tale by

RONALD SEARLE

THE STEPHEN GREENE PRESS

Library of Congress Catalog Card Number: 73-173406
International Standard Book Number: 0-8289-0149-x
Published in the United States of America by
The Stephen Greene Press, Brattleboro, Vermont 05301
Printed in Great Britain